Introduction

For this, my seventh book in the series I have chosen Darnall, but as I have sor photographs of old Darnall that I could not possibly have taken since they date fr acknowledge my debt to those photographers of the past.

There are some of my own photographs interspersed - you can usually spot these by the later date.

Darnall has not produced many celebrities. William Walker whose house is in the book, was believed to have been the executioner of Charles the First. Charlie Peace is the best known Victorian murderer after Jack the Ripper. He lived in Darnall. The Duke of Darnall is affectionately remembered for his pretensions of grandeur. He was often seen in Sheffield helpfully directing traffic where no help was required. He could be a nuisance but he is remembered with affection. He too is in the book.

At the time of writing I hear that Darnall is to be given a make-over. If that is to be so this little book will be a useful record of how things used to be. Already much that is shown here has disappeared. Once the "improvers" have had their way I fear much more will have gone.

I hope the book brings happy memories to the people of old Darnall.

INDEX

Balfour Road 32
Blacksmith, Village 39
Bowden Houstead Woods 73
Britannia Road 44
Bus Museum 41
Catcliffe Road 67, 70
Chelmsford Street 15
Cinemas 51, 67
Craven Road 40
Darnall Hall 74
Darnall Medical Aid 3, 4
Darnall Old Hall 68, 69
Darnall Public Hall 79
Darnall Road 32, 42, 47, 63
Darnall School 5
Darnall Station 30, 31
Darnall Terminus 26
Duke of Darnall 66
Dunkirk Square 53
Fisher Lane 46
Greenland Road 41, 64
Handsworth Road 10, 49, 75
Helen Road 76
High Hazels Park 9, 48
Industry Road 65
Irving Street 74
Little Attercliffe 34, 35
Main Road 11, 21, 22, 23, 25, 33, 36, 37, 38, 45, 50, 51, 52, 53, 54, 55, 56, 57, 58, 59, 60, 61, 62, 78, 80
Owler Greave Road 8
Peace, Charlie 43, 44
Prince of Wales Road 66, 71, 72, 77
Roundel Street 12
Staniforth Road 6, 7, 13, 14, 15, 16, 17, 18, 19, 20, 21, 22, 23, 26
Station Road 24, 25, 26, 27, 28, 29
Tesco Stores 80

Darnall Medical aid was an annual event to raise money for local hospitals in the days before the National Health Service. Here Dick Turpin was a prize-winner.

Another example of a Darnall Medical Aid entrant but this time all the effort has gone onto the horse - a magnificent animal belonging to a coal merchant.

Darnall School around 1906. There was strict segregation between the boys and the girls after the age of seven. If you look at the old schools that survive you can still see the entrances for “Girls” and “Boys”.

Staniforth Road between Garth Road and Wilfrid Road.Standing outside the Brightside and Carbrook Co-op is one of those little economy cars that would take you to Blackpool and back on a gallon of petrol.

The Balfour cinema was on Staniforth Road. The building still stands, but is now in use as a carpet shop. It is still possible to see the original roof and projection cubicle inside the shop. It opened in 1913 as The Darnall Picture Palace becoming The Balfour in 1933. It closed as a cinema on 28th February 1959 with two films: *Winchester 73* and *East of Java*.

Owler Greave Road was swallowed up when Prince of Wales Road was built in 1936.
See page 77 for a later view of these buildings shortly before demolition.

High Hazels paddling pool when such things were allowed.
Now they have all been drained, which is a pity.

The bottom of Handsworth Hill looking towards the timbered wall of the Rose and Crown.
The girls in pinafores indicate the date as, possibly, Edwardian (1901 to 1910)

Silver Jubilee celebrations for George V, in 1935 with bunting adorning the Meadow Inn at 81 Main Street, Darnall

Roundel Street is nearer to Attercliffe than Darnall but the photograph shows the entrance to another disappearing phenomenon - the Working Men's Club. This one being the Attercliffe Radical Club. The date is 1974.

No. 56 Staniforth Road was Ashworth's chippy. I was spotted taking my photograph back in May 1974 but I hope it will bring back pleasant memories to the Ashworths.

These shops on Staniforth Road were above Roundel Street and below Palmer Street. The date is 1981.

Staniforth Road at Chelmsford Street, again in May 1974. Shoe repair shops are now very few in number. Modern soles seem to outlast the uppers. Leather was comfortable but wore very quickly.

Staniforth Road below the railway bridge. This is a difficult one to date. My guess would be the early 1920s.

Staniforth Road in 1981 above Balfour Road. On the left are the Cravens Works currently under threat. On the right one of the fast disappearing independent filling station and beyond can just be seen the Balfour cinema.

A view down Staniforth Road taken in 1981. The filling station is the one on the previous picture.

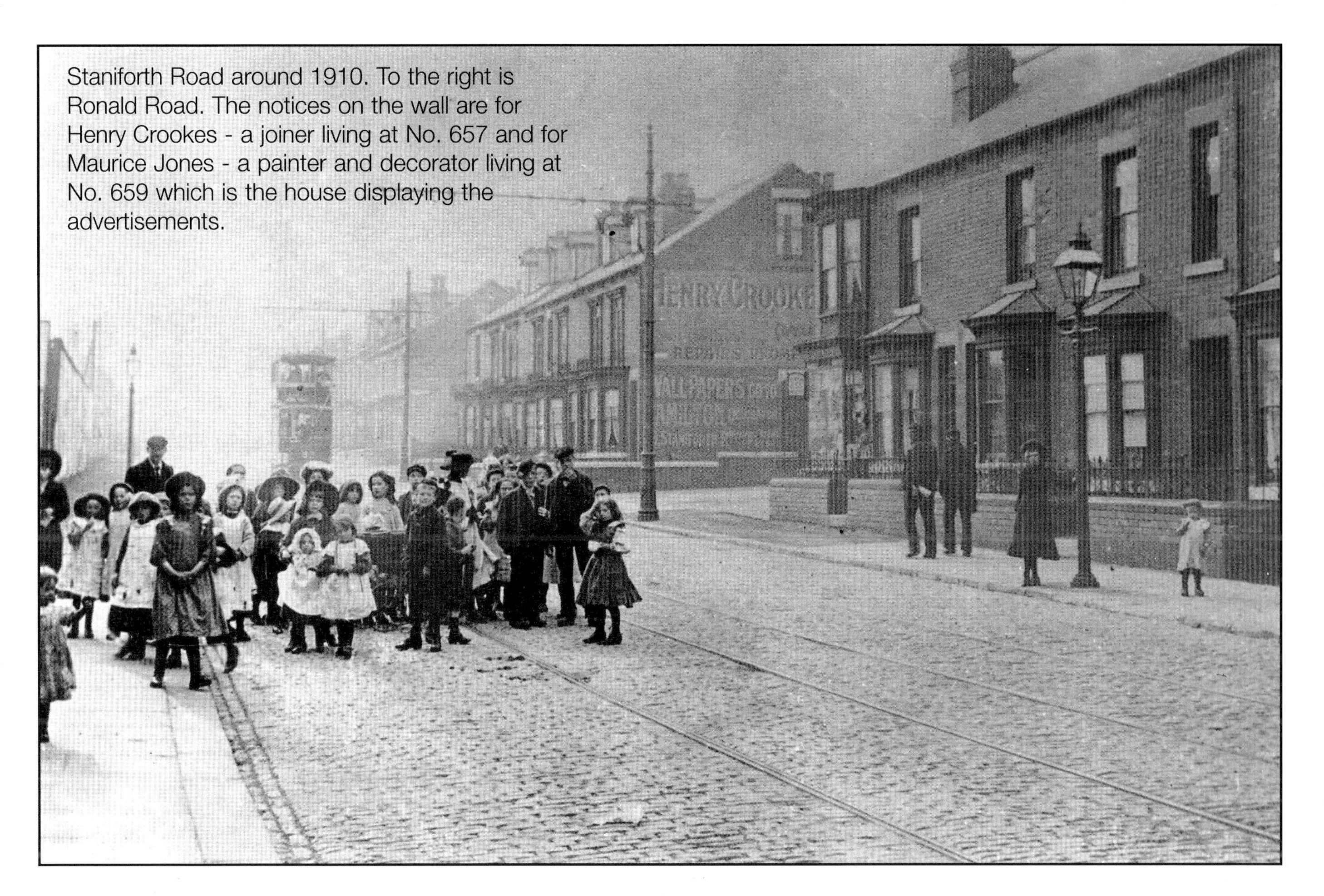

Staniforth Road around 1910. To the right is Ronald Road. The notices on the wall are for Henry Crookes - a joiner living at No. 657 and for Maurice Jones - a painter and decorator living at No. 659 which is the house displaying the advertisements.

This view of Staniforth Road dates from 1981.
The lone person is heading towards the elegant Darnall Horticultural Club at the corner of Gainsford Road.

This is where Main Road joins Staniforth Road around 1912. Every shop has its awning - another sight that has now virtually disappeared. Metal grills are now a more common feature.

This shows Staniforth Road where it joins Main Road as it was in 1981. Most of the shops have now changed hands.

Here Staniforth Road meets Main Road. It was the site of the old tram terminus though when this was taken in 1981 tramcars were a twenty-year old memory. We little thought they would make a come-back.

This shows the shop at the corner of Station Road before the First World War. Its interest lies not so much in the empty shop as as in the onlookers.

Holy Trinity Church stands at the corner of Station Road and Main Road. It was built in 1840 but not consecrated until 1845. It was enlarged in 1889.

The picture says it all except the date which I estimate to be around 1912.

The empty shop on page 24 has been replaced. The new shop is here occupied by the Public Benefit Company. Didn't anyone wear shoes in those days.

On Station Road stands this elegant school dating from the early days of the Sheffield School Board in the 1870s. It was linked to the Holy Trinity Church nearby.

Looking down Station Road in 1982 the buildings on the left have since been cleared to give a better view of Holy Trinity church school. See the previous page.

This was Station Road in 1905. The photographer was standing with his back to the station looking towards the church. The event was the visit of Edward VII and Alexandra to open the new University on Western Bank. On the left of the picture houses were demolished to make a car park for the station.

Darnall Station in its golden days. It is still in use with a car park on Station Road.

An express steam train passing through Darnall Station. This is a difficult one to date. My guess would be somewhere around 1914.

Around 1898 Mrs Fayram and Miss Bottom pose outside their shop at the corner of Balfour Road and Darnall Rd. See the next picture to see how they changed in the next thirty-odd years,

The same ladies around 1930 having moved to 170 Main Road into what seems to be a second-hand clothes busines..

Little Attercliffe was an area bounded by Darnall Road, Balfour Road, Shirland Lane and Bawtry Road. The entrance to the small hamlet was approached from Darnall Road.

Another photograph of Little Attercliffe. If you study the two together you can see how they were situated.
These cottages are in the distance on the previous page.

Main Road at Mandeville Street with, at No. 81, the Meadow Inn on the right.
I do not have a date but I estimate it to be around 1912.

This was how Main Road looked back in 1905.

The notice tells all except the date which was around 1912 but how about hygiene?

"Behold - a giant am I". The Darnall village blacksmith, Mr Woodhead, poses in front of his partly demolished shop with an admiring group of onlookers. Inset is the shop that was near the old tram terminus.

Jesse Fuller's boot repair shop was to be found at No. 107 Craven Road - the last house before Surrey Road.
Notice that he wasn't interested in such fripperies as shoes.

Sheffield bus museum was situated on Greenland Road. This occasion was an open day held on the 10th August 1985. The buses are now housed in cramped premises at the junction of Weedon Street and Attercliffe Common in the old horse-tram sheds.

The magnificent Ball Inn stands on Darnall Road. Its splendid architecture reflects the days of King Edward VII and indeed the date 1904 is carried on the central arch. Alas, I fear for its future.

This effigy of Charlie Peace in the original police cell at West Bar that he occupied after his arrest can now be seen at the Fire Museum. He was living on Britannia Road, Darnall when he murdered Mr Dyson. He was later hung at Armley gaol in Leeds. Also visible are his pistol and his spectacles.

This view of Britannia Road taken in 1964 is interesting because it shows the house in which Sheffield's most notorious criminal, Charlie Peace lived at the time that he murdered Mr Dyson. The Dysons lived in a house just above Charlie who had been pestering Mrs Dyson to such an extent that they moved to Banner Cross. Undeterred, Charlie tracked them down and murdered the husband. His house was the third from the left. All have now gone.

This was originally The Bradley Well pub but was closed in the 1990s to be re-born as the Terminus Tavern. It stands on Main Road at No. 150.
Inset: The original Bradley Well pub being demolished in 1910.

Fisher Lane was an undeveloped lane or footpath in 1903 - that was before the new school was built. Here, dominating the picture is the caretaker's house with its own gate. It is a pity that now many schools do not have a caretaker on the premises. It would obviate the devastating fences that surround them like so may prisons.

The Sportsman Inn on Darnall Road was caught on an unusually pleasant day in early April. I estimate the pub must be around a century old by now. St. George's Day is about to be celebrated.

High Hazels Park museum is no longer open as such but is now a golf clubhouse.

The picture, top left, shows the old Museum in its heyday. The two pictures, top right, show it in use, present day, as the Tinsley Golf Clubhouse.

The bottom two pictures show the park being enjoyed by local residents on a warm spring day.

A view of Darnall taken from the bottom of Handsworth Hill around 1920.

This group of shops on Main Road were, from right to left, Nos 13-15 Marriott's leather merchants, No. 9 Thurman's beer-off shop, No. 7 Don Valley cleaners, No. 5 Mosley's record shop, No. 3 Bingham's barber's shop. The date is 1965.

The last days of the Lyric Cinema on Main Road. It was situated between Nos. 98 and 108. The photograph was taken in 1983.The cinema which was opened in 1920 closed as a cinema in 1962. For a time in survived as a Bingo hall but finally gave up the ghost shortly after this picture was taken.

The Duke of York pub stands at 135 Main Road. Catley Road is to the left.The building has all the hallmarks of a late Edwardian hotel. The crane is busy building the new another supermarket and the year was 1983. Darnall Old Hall (see pages 68 & 69) stood where the "Costcutter" building stands.

Dunkirk cottages. Dunkirk Square was to be found off Main Road between numbers 165 and 171.

These shops are from 1983. They number from 150 and upwards on Main Road towards Staniforth Road. Already the nature of the shops is beginning to change. On the right, MICAR is catering for the rapidly growing body of motor car owners.

Main Road in 1965. The shops were: 170 Lawler - butcher; 172 Doris Miller - confectioner; 174-6 Davy's - provisions; 178 Parish - newsagents; 180 Smith - fruiterer; 182 Wesley's Pet & fisherman's Store; 186 - Carousel Cafe; 188 Jas Coombes - boots and shoes; 190 Dawson Bros - furnishing fabrics.

A great photograph of the shops on Main Road in 1907. The numbers run from 174 to 186.
It is remarkable that the Parish family are present on this and the previous picture - a period of almost sixty years.

A snapshot taken on Main Road near Staniforth Road in 1981.
Nos. 180 and above.

Hiram Cheetham, greengrocer had his shop at 197 Main Road. It would seem he also had a nice line in garden supplies. He is listed in my 1905 and 1915 directories but had been replaced by 1925.

The National Westminster Bank was at No. 197 Main Road. In the distance is the road to Handsworth.

Hill's Forage merchant's were to be found at 203 Main Road. Inset is a photograph of Mr Hill with his horse and cart. The date is around 1930.

Main Road at Wellington Place. The Wellington pub is at No. 222. It is reputed to have the ghost of a former pub owner. The photograph dates from 1981.
On the left behind the bus is the Rose and Crown pub.

Main Road, Court 15 as it was in 1963. This must have been near the terminus.

The Old Cricket Ground pub stood at No. 371 Darnall Road. The road to the right is Vine Road.
Here is a problem. The road to the right is called Florence Street on my 1903 map. By 1915 it is Vine Road.

It is hard to believe that this photograph of Greenland farm could be anywhere near the present Greenland Road but so it was. The date is estimated to be 1892.

Industry Road is shown in the Edwardian era when the visit of a photographer was a big event as witness the interest shown by all the kids.

The Duke of Darnall is on the left. He was a familiar figure in the City Centre in the '40s and '50s - always with his bowler hat.
Back in those days I think he enjoyed his celebrity status.

This is not a particularly inspiring picture of a tram passing down Prince of Wales Road only notable in being the first to make the journey back in 1936.

The Cinema House, Darnall was on Catcliffe Road.
It was quite small seating only around 500. It opened in 1913 and closed in 1957.

Darnall Old Hall had the date 1702 over the door but was built in 1580.The number was 147 (Main Rd.) and it stood at the side of the Duke of York pub.

It is a tradition that this was William Walker's house. Walker is held to have been the executioner of King Charles the First who was beheaded on 30th January 1649.

Darnall Old Hall:
Left: The doorway and lintel.

Right: The Allsop family taken in 1905.

See page 52 for the location of this old hall.

This is Catcliffe Road where the end of Britannia Road joins it. The date was 1963 but the tiny house cum shop was a throw-back to the hungry thirties when many a terreced house owner took to shop-keeping. By the time this photo was taken it had reverted to its domestic status.

These cottages were situated on what is now Prince of Wales Road.

This is how Prince of Wales Road looked in 1926. Noticeable is the number of people out for a stroll. Presumably this was still Main Road before the Prince of Wales officially opened the new road that was to receive his name.

This photograph was taken shortly after the opening - around 1926 of the new open-air swimming pool in Bowden Houstead Woods.

Darnall Hall. This building became the Liberal Club in 1908.
It was situated on Irving Street.

This is Handsworth Hill viewed from Darnall in 1968. W.H. Curtis on the left was a well-known electrical store that was eventually closed in face of increasing competition from the big retailers.

Helen Road was to be found running parallel to Industry Road above Darnall Cemetery off Surrey Road.
The photograph carries the date 1910.
All this has now gone.

Prince of Wales Road as it was around 1960.

This is Main Road at Prince of Wales Road in 1983. On the right the Tesco Supermarket is visible (see page 80) and on the other side of the road is the Wellington pub (see page 61). Prince of Wales Road runs off to the left.

Darnall Public Hall in all its newly built spleandour back in Edwardian days.

Back in the 1960s supermarkets were a novelty.
We little realised then how they would come to dominate our lives.
This was taken shortly after the opening of this modest Tesco branch back in 1968. The location is 215 Main Road.